Echoes of Inheritance

Lamarck's Lasting Legacy in Psychological Thought

Freudian Trips

Copyright Page

© 2024 by Freudian Trips

All rights reserved. No part of this book may be reproduced in any form or by any electronic or mechanical means, including information storage and retrieval systems, without permission in writing from the publisher, except by a reviewer who may quote brief passages in a review.

This book is a work of non-fiction. Unless otherwise noted, the author and the publisher make no explicit guarantees as to the accuracy of the information contained in this book and will not be held responsible for any errors or omissions.

Published by Omniterra Media Inc

First Edition

Visit the author's website at www.freudiantrips.com

Introduction: Setting the Stage

A Journey Begins with Jean-Baptiste Lamarck

Imagine living in a world where the more you stretch to reach the higher leaves as a giraffe, the longer your neck grows—and then, your offspring inherit your newly elongated neck. This scenario captures the essence of an idea proposed over two centuries ago by a French scientist named Jean-Baptiste Lamarck. Born in 1744, Lamarck was one of the first to suggest a theory that traits acquired during an organism's lifetime could be passed on to the next generation, a concept he called the inheritance of acquired characteristics.

Lamarck's theories came at a time when the world was just beginning to embrace the scientific study of life. He believed that organisms adapt to their environments, and these changes are then inherited by their offspring. For example, he speculated that blacksmiths, through their work, developed stronger muscles, which they then passed on to their children.

The Reception of a Revolutionary Idea

When Lamarck introduced his ideas, the scientific community was intrigued but skeptical. This was a bold shift from the static view of life that many held at the time. Initially, his concepts were met with curiosity and for some, excitement, as they offered a new way to understand the ever-changing nature of life. However, as more was learned about biology, skepticism grew. The idea that physical changes within an organism's lifetime could directly affect the genetic material passed to the next generation lacked empirical support and was eventually overshadowed by the genetic laws discovered by Gregor Mendel, which formed the basis of modern genetics.

Despite the lack of scientific backing, Lamarck's ideas sparked conversations and influenced thinking across various fields, including psychology.

From Biology to Psychology: A Theoretical Migration

As the dust settled on Lamarck's theories in biology, an interesting transition occurred; his ideas began to seep into the realm of psychology. Psychologists started wondering if behaviors learned by parents through experience could somehow be transmitted to their children. The notion was appealing—it suggested that not just physical traits but also acquired knowledge and skills could be inherited.

This migration of ideas was particularly prominent in the early days of psychological theory when scientists were still mapping out the vast terrains of the human mind. Lamarckian inheritance offered a framework to explore how environmental influences could shape behavioral traits across generations. It opened up discussions on the potential for cultural and social

Disclaimer

The views and opinions expressed in this book are those of the author(s) and do not necessarily reflect the official policy or position of any other agency, organization, employer, or company. The contents of this book are for informational and educational purposes only and are not intended to serve as professional advice, diagnosis, or treatment.

The information provided in this book is believed to be accurate and reliable as of the date of publication. However, it may include some errors or inaccuracies, and no warranty or guarantee is provided regarding the accuracy, timeliness, or applicability of the content.

Readers are encouraged to consult with professional philosophers, educators, or other qualified professionals where appropriate for personalized advice. The author(s) and publisher shall not be liable for any loss, damage, or harm caused or alleged to be caused, directly or indirectly, by the

information or ideas contained, suggested, or referenced in
this book.

By reading this book, the reader acknowledges and agrees
that they are solely responsible for how they interpret and
apply the information contained herein.

This book may also include references to other works, studies,
and sources. These references are provided for further
reading and exploration and do not imply endorsement or
validation of the specific theories, viewpoints, or
interpretations presented in those works.

traits, such as language, customs, and even emotional responses, to be passed down from parents to children.

While modern genetics has shown that Lamarck's biological model of inheritance is not generally applicable, the psychological community has not entirely let go of the notion. Concepts reminiscent of Lamarckian inheritance still appear in discussions about the effects of environment on psychological development and the intergenerational transmission of behaviors and traits.

A Legacy Reconsidered

As we dive deeper into this book, we'll explore how these early ideas have evolved and found new life in contemporary psychological theories. From the intriguing world of epigenetics to the study of neuroplasticity, we'll see how echoes of Lamarck's legacy still reverberate in modern science. Our journey through the chapters will unravel how an idea, once thought to be obsolete, continues to influence our understanding of human behavior and development.

This introduction sets the stage for a journey through time and thought, exploring how the seeds planted by Lamarck have grown in unexpected ways, shaping not just our understanding of biology, but also the complex world of psychological science.

Chapter 1: Foundations of Lamarckian Thought in Psychology

The Man Behind the Theory

Jean-Baptiste Lamarck was born in northern France in 1744 into a modest family. Despite his humble beginnings, Lamarck's intellectual curiosity and dedication to learning propelled him into the world of science. Originally setting out for a military career, an injury shifted his path towards medicine and botany. His fascination with the natural world led him to the prestigious position of a professor of botany at the Jardin des Plantes in Paris. Here, his work took a revolutionary turn as he delved into the study of evolution.

Lamarck's most notable contribution to science is his evolutionary theory, particularly the idea that organisms evolve over time by adapting to their environments. He proposed that traits acquired to adapt, such as a blacksmith's muscular arms or the stretched neck of a giraffe reaching for higher leaves, could be passed on to offspring. This was a groundbreaking thought because it suggested that life was not static but dynamic, continually transforming with each passing generation.

A Time of Scientific Awakening

The early 19th century was a period of immense scientific exploration and discovery. Scholars and naturalists were traveling the globe, discovering new species and questioning long-held beliefs about the natural world. It was a time when the foundations of biology as we know it were just being laid down.

In this environment, Lamarck's ideas were both radical and intriguing. They challenged the prevailing notion of an unchanging world that had been largely accepted since the days of Aristotle. Lamarck argued against this static view, proposing instead that life is in a constant state of flux, driven by the needs of organisms to adapt to their environments.

His ideas came at a time when Europe was buzzing with new ideas about democracy, individual rights, and scientific progress. Lamarck's theories resonated with the spirit of the age, which was all about change and improvement.

From Biology to Psychology: How Lamarck Inspired Minds

While Lamarck's biological theories began to wane in the face of emerging genetic evidence, they found a new home in the burgeoning field of psychology. In the late 19th and early 20th centuries, as psychologists sought to understand the human mind and behavior, Lamarckian ideas provided a useful framework. Psychologists pondered whether learned behaviors could also be passed down to future generations, influencing how people think, act, and feel.

This transition was not just about inheriting physical traits but also about the inheritance of emotional and intellectual dispositions. Could the resilience shown by a mother in adversity be inherited by her child? Could the learned fears or prejudices of a father find their way into the psyche of his descendants? These were the types of questions that Lamarckian psychology aimed to answer.

In this new context, Lamarck's ideas were transformed to fit psychological phenomena, extending his influence far beyond what he might have imagined. As psychologists began to study the impact of environment and experience on human behavior, Lamarckian theory offered a compelling narrative that behaviors and emotional responses shaped by personal experiences could have deeper roots in previous generations.

Thus, the foundations of Lamarckian thought in psychology were laid, built upon the intriguing proposals of Jean-Baptiste Lamarck. His ideas, though rooted in the study of plants and animals, evolved into concepts that would one day seek to explain the complexities of human behavior and cognition. This chapter has traced the journey of these ideas from their biological beginnings to their psychological applications, showing how they have continued to influence thought and theory in unexpected ways.

Chapter 2: Lamarckian Psychology in the 19th and Early 20th Centuries

Seeds of Influence

As we venture further into the history of psychological thought, it becomes clear that the tendrils of Lamarck's ideas have woven themselves deeply into the fabric of early psychology. During the 19th and early 20th centuries, when psychology was still separating itself from philosophy and biology to stand as its own discipline, Jean-Baptiste Lamarck's theories offered an intriguing explanation for how behaviors and mental attributes could be passed from one generation to the next.

Pioneers and Their Psychological Explorations

Several forward-thinking psychologists and theorists found Lamarck's ideas particularly compelling. They speculated that not only physical traits but also learned behaviors and psychological characteristics could be inherited. This section delves into a few case studies of these pioneering psychologists:

1. **James Mark Baldwin** - Often associated with the concept of "Baldwin Effect," which has parallels to Lamarckian inheritance, Baldwin proposed that learned behaviors could indirectly influence evolution. He suggested that if a behavior, beneficial to survival, is learned and repeatedly taught, it could lead to genetic changes over generations, thus mirroring Lamarck's idea of traits becoming ingrained and passed down.
2. **Sigmund Freud** - While not a strict Lamarckian, Freud's theories of psychoanalysis hint at Lamarckian influence. For instance, he discussed the concept of inherited memory, suggesting that certain memories and experiences from one's ancestors could influence an individual's unconscious mind and behaviors.
3. **Ivan Pavlov** - Known for his work on conditioned reflexes, Pavlov did not directly advocate for Lamarckian inheritance but his research on behavioral conditioning raised questions about whether such learned behaviors could be transmitted to offspring, a hypothesis that resonates with Lamarckian themes.

The Psychological Tapestry of Lamarckian Threads

Beyond individual theorists, Lamarckian psychology influenced broader psychological concepts, particularly the inheritance of phobias and acquired skills. This segment explores how these ideas were thought to be transmitted from parents to children:

- **Inheritance of Phobias**: The theory suggested that if a parent developed a phobia during their lifetime—

say, a fear of snakes due to a traumatic encounter—
this intense fear could be passed down to the child.
This concept proposed a direct transmission of
acquired traits, aligning closely with Lamarckian
inheritance.

- **Acquired Skills**: Similarly, it was hypothesized that
skills acquired by parents, such as musical ability or
linguistic prowess, could be more easily learned by
their children. This was thought to be due to some
form of psychological preparation in the child, making
them more adept at these skills.

Analysis and Reflection

While these theories provided fascinating insights and
prompted further research, they also faced significant
challenges. The rise of genetics and Mendelian inheritance
began to cast doubt on the Lamarckian mechanisms, leading
to skepticism about the direct inheritance of acquired traits.
Despite this, the early 20th century was a time of exploration
and debate, and Lamarckian psychology contributed
significantly to the dialogue around heredity and behavior.

The period also saw critical discussion and experimentation,
which, although it did not always confirm Lamarckian ideas,
undoubtedly enriched the psychological sciences by pushing
boundaries and challenging researchers to think differently
about the origins and mechanisms of human behavior.

As we conclude this chapter, it's clear that while not all of
Lamarck's ideas were embraced or proven by later scientific
standards, his influence on early psychological theories
provided a fertile ground for discussion and hypothesis. These

early psychological explorations into the inheritance of acquired characteristics paved the way for more nuanced understandings of genetics, behavior, and the legacy of our ancestors' experiences in shaping who we are today. The journey through Lamarckian psychology shows a field in transition, grappling with the complexities of mind and behavior across generations.

Chapter 3: The Decline of Lamarckism in Light of Modern Genetics

A New Chapter in Understanding Heredity

As the 20th century progressed, the world of science witnessed revolutionary changes that reshaped our understanding of how traits are passed from one generation to the next. At the heart of this transformation was the rediscovery of the work of Gregor Mendel, an Austrian monk whose experiments with pea plants laid the foundation for what we now call Mendelian genetics.

Mendelian Genetics Takes the Stage

Mendel's work, initially overlooked, gained prominence at the turn of the century and quickly overshadowed Lamarck's theories. Mendel demonstrated through his meticulous breeding experiments that traits are inherited according to specific patterns. These patterns reflected the segregation and assortment of discrete units of inheritance, later known as genes. Mendel's findings suggested that traits are passed through defined genetic mechanisms, which seemed to leave little room for the idea that acquired characteristics could be inherited as Lamarck had proposed.

The Modern Evolutionary Synthesis

The nail in the coffin for Lamarckism came with the development of the modern evolutionary synthesis in the mid-20th century. This powerful theory combined Mendelian genetics with Darwinian natural selection, providing a comprehensive framework that explained how evolution occurs over generations without the need for the inheritance of acquired traits. It illustrated that genetic mutations and recombination, followed by natural selection, were sufficient to account for evolutionary change, further marginalizing Lamarckian ideas in biology.

Lamarckian Inheritance Faces Challenges

As genetics continued to advance, particularly with the discovery of the structure of DNA by Watson and Crick in 1953, the mechanisms of heredity became clearer. DNA was shown to be the material that carries genetic information, firmly establishing that traits are inherited through genetic codes, not through changes acquired in an organism's lifetime. These developments made it increasingly difficult to sustain the idea that physical changes due to environment or behavior could be directly passed down to offspring.

Yet, Lamarckian Ideas Persist in Psychology

Despite these significant scientific advancements, the allure of Lamarckian ideas did not completely vanish, especially in the field of psychology. Psychologists were intrigued by the possibility that behavioral adaptations and psychological changes influenced by the environment could somehow be transmitted across generations. This interest was not merely theoretical; it had practical implications in understanding patterns of behavior, psychological traits, and mental health issues within families.

The persistence of Lamarckian ideas in psychology can be partly explained by the complexity of human behavior and the evident influence of both genetics and environment on psychological development. For instance, the concept of epigenetics—changes in gene expression caused by mechanisms other than changes in the underlying DNA sequence—offered a kind of modern-day echo of Lamarckian inheritance. These changes can indeed be influenced by the environment and, in some cases, passed to the next generation, providing a biological basis for some of the intergenerational transmission of traits and behaviors.

Reflections and Moving Forward

The decline of Lamarckism in the face of modern genetics does not mark the end of its relevance or its contribution to science. Instead, it highlights the dynamic nature of scientific inquiry—where old ideas are tested against new evidence, sometimes discarded, but often reshaped and integrated into broader understandings. In psychology, the spirit of Lamarck's ideas continues to inspire research into how the environment and individual experiences might shape not just one, but successive generations.

This chapter reflects on how Lamarck's legacy, while challenged and transformed by the advances in genetics, still plays a role in our quest to understand the complex interactions between our genetic makeup and our environments. The journey of Lamarckian thought through the ages underscores the richness and adaptability of scientific ideas, even as we advance toward ever more sophisticated understandings of heredity and evolution.

Chapter 4: Contemporary Perspectives on Lamarckian Psychology

A New Era for Old Ideas

While Jean-Baptiste Lamarck's theories were set aside in the biological sciences, intriguing parallels have emerged in contemporary psychology that reflect a transformed understanding of his ideas. Today, the fields of neuroplasticity and epigenetics show us that our environment can indeed influence how our brain works and even how our genes operate, suggesting that Lamarck's notion of acquired characteristics isn't as far off as once thought—at least, when it comes to behavior and psychological traits.

Neuroplasticity: The Brain's Ability to Adapt

Neuroplasticity refers to the brain's capacity to reorganize itself through the establishment of novel neural connections throughout an individual's lifespan. This adaptability allows the brain to recover from injuries, adapt to new situations, or learn new information. The concept of neuroplasticity echoes Lamarckian ideas in the way it emphasizes the potential for life experiences to cause lasting changes in the brain. For instance, learning a new language or mastering a musical instrument can physically alter the brain's structure, enhancing areas responsible for these skills.

Epigenetics: Bridging Experience and Genetics

Epigenetics involves changes in gene expression that do not involve alterations to the genetic code itself but are influenced by environmental factors. These changes can sometimes be passed down to the next generation, providing a modern parallel to Lamarckian inheritance. For example, studies have shown that trauma can lead to epigenetic changes that may affect not only the person who experienced the trauma but also their offspring, potentially making them more susceptible to stress or fear.

Case Studies in Modern Research

To further illustrate how contemporary psychology revisits Lamarckian themes, let's explore a few case studies:

1. **The Dutch Hunger Winter Study**: Researchers studied individuals conceived during the 1944-1945 Dutch Hunger Winter, a time of severe famine. They found that these individuals, decades later, had different epigenetic markers compared to their siblings who were not conceived during the famine. This study suggests that environmental conditions experienced by one generation can physically influence the next.
2. **Learning and Memory in Rats**: In experiments where mother rats were taught to navigate mazes, their offspring also showed a quicker aptitude for maze-

learning, even without direct interaction with their mothers. This suggests that some aspects of learning and memory might be influenced by what the previous generation encountered.

3. **Trauma and Resilience Studies**: Ongoing research into how the children of trauma survivors often show heightened anxiety or stress responses suggests that psychological impacts might have heritable components that align with Lamarckian ideas.

Reflections on Modern Lamarckian Psychology

These modern developments suggest that while Lamarck's original theories about the physical inheritance of traits may not hold in their original form, his broader ideas about the impact of the environment on an organism and its descendants resonate in new ways in contemporary psychological research. This opens up exciting possibilities for understanding how the experiences of one generation can influence the next, not through direct genetic transmission, but through the plasticity of the brain and epigenetic modifications.

As we continue to explore the intersection of environment, behavior, and genetics, it becomes clear that Lamarckian themes are far from obsolete. Instead, they offer a rich framework for understanding the complex interplay between our genes and our experiences. In this chapter, we've seen that Lamarck's legacy, though transformed and updated with new scientific understanding, continues to influence psychological science, encouraging us to think deeply about how we are shaped by the lives of those who came before us.

Chapter 5: Lamarckian Inheritance and Educational Psychology

Lamarck in the Classroom

The influence of Jean-Baptiste Lamarck extends beyond the natural sciences and into the realm of education, where his ideas about the acquisition and transmission of traits offer compelling insights into how we learn and teach. While we now understand that genetic changes do not occur as Lamarck once proposed, the metaphorical application of his theories to education suggests that the environments we create and the experiences we provide can deeply influence not only individual learners but potentially future generations as well.

Applying Lamarckian Ideas to Learning and Education

In the educational context, Lamarckian inheritance can be seen as a model for understanding how acquired knowledge and skills might be passed on not through genes, but through culture, shared practices, and continuous learning environments. For instance, when a generation of students learns to integrate technology effectively in their learning process, they are likely to pass on these skills and the value they find in them to the next generation, thus 'inheriting' a transformed educational landscape.

Neo-Lamarckian Approaches in Education

A neo-Lamarckian approach to education would emphasize the importance of environment and experience in shaping student outcomes. This perspective encourages educators and policymakers to consider how educational environments and teaching methods can be designed to enhance learning effectively and inclusively. Such approaches might include:

- **Personalized Learning**: Tailoring education to fit individual student needs, abilities, and learning styles, ensuring that each student can acquire the skills they need in the most effective way.
- **Emotional and Social Learning**: Incorporating lessons that help students manage emotions and develop social skills, which are crucial for personal and professional success and can be culturally transmitted to enrich community interactions.

Implications for Educational Practices and Policies

Adopting a neo-Lamarckian approach in educational settings suggests several policy implications:

- **Investment in Early Education**: Early childhood experiences have profound impacts on later success.

Investing in high-quality early education could ensure that beneficial adaptations are 'acquired' as early as possible.

- **Lifelong Learning**: Promoting continuous education through life reflects the idea that learning is not confined to early years but is a continuous process that adapts and evolves across a lifetime.
- **Cultural Transmission**: Recognizing that cultural practices and values are transmitted through education, policies might focus on preserving and passing on cultural heritage and practices through school curriculums.

Theoretical Exploration of Generational Outcomes

Exploring how acquired knowledge and skills influence generations requires us to look at long-term educational outcomes and societal changes. If one generation values critical thinking and problem-solving, its emphasis in education could lead to broader societal shifts in these areas, affecting how future generations think, learn, and solve problems.

Lamarckian Inheritance Beyond Genetics

In conclusion, while Lamarck's genetic theories may not apply to modern biology, his ideas inspire a broader interpretation in educational psychology. They encourage us to consider how the educational environments we foster today can influence not just our immediate learners but also shape the predispositions and capacities of future generations. Through this lens, educators and policymakers are reminded of the significant, lasting impact their work can have, inspiring a thoughtful approach to how we teach, learn, and grow together in a continually evolving educational landscape.

Chapter 6: The Future of Lamarckian Ideas in Psychological Science

Embracing a Future Inspired by the Past

As we explore the evolving landscape of psychological science, it becomes evident that the ideas first posited by Jean-Baptiste Lamarck continue to influence modern thought, albeit in nuanced and complex ways. Looking forward, the integration of Lamarckian principles with contemporary psychological research promises to open new avenues for understanding human behavior and mental processes.

Integrating Lamarckian Ideas into Modern Psychological Research

Future research might explore how environmental changes influence psychological development across generations more deeply. For instance, could significant cultural shifts—like the digital revolution—alter cognitive structures in ways that might be passed down to future generations, even if not genetically? Lamarckian ideas suggest that adaptations to such environments could manifest in subsequent generations through behavioral changes, possibly supported by epigenetic mechanisms.

Interdisciplinary Approaches: Blending Old Ideas with New Science

One of the most exciting prospects for future research is the potential for interdisciplinary approaches that blend genetics, psychology, and Lamarckian principles. This could involve:

- **Epigenetic Psychology**: Studying how gene expression is affected by individual experiences and how these changes might influence behaviors or predispositions in offspring.
- **Cultural Psychology and Sociology**: Exploring how cultural practices and social behaviors, once thought to be learned only through social interaction, might also involve biological components that affect gene expression.
- **Environmental Psychology**: Examining how long-term changes in the environment could shape psychological traits in a population over time.

These interdisciplinary efforts could help us understand the complex interactions between our genetic makeup, our environments, and our behaviors in more holistic ways.

The Role of Technology in Future Research

Advancements in technology, such as brain imaging and genetic sequencing, will play a crucial role in future research. These tools could provide the necessary data to explore the potential biological underpinnings of learned behaviors and their transmission. For example, by using longitudinal studies that track brain changes alongside behavioral changes, researchers could uncover patterns that hint at Lamarckian mechanisms.

Final Thoughts on Lamarck's Legacy

As we speculate on the future of psychological science, it is clear that Jean-Baptiste Lamarck's legacy is not only enduring but also evolving. His ideas, once revolutionary and later contested, have found a new resonance in an age that seeks to understand the complex interplay of genes and environment. Lamarck's vision of a dynamic, adaptable natural world now encourages psychologists to think more broadly about how humans adapt to rapidly changing environments.

In conclusion, while Lamarckian genetics as originally proposed may not have stood the test of time, the themes of adaptation and inheritance continue to influence psychological science in profound ways. As we advance, the spirit of Lamarck's ideas encourages ongoing curiosity and exploration, reminding us that science is never static but a continually evolving dialogue between the past and the present, aiming to illuminate the future. Through this lens, Lamarck's ideas will likely continue to inspire and challenge psychological research, offering valuable insights into the nature of human development and the legacy we leave for future generations.

Conclusion: Reevaluating Lamarck

A Journey Through Lamarck's Legacy

As we conclude our exploration of Jean-Baptiste Lamarck's influence on psychological thought, it's important to reflect on the key points discussed throughout this book. We began with an introduction to Lamarck, his life, and his revolutionary ideas about the inheritance of acquired characteristics. We saw how these ideas initially captivated the scientific community of the early 19th century, despite the lack of empirical support that would later lead to their decline in the realm of biology.

From Biology to Psychology: A Legacy Transformed

Our journey took us through the migration of Lamarckian thought from biology into the nascent field of psychology, where his ideas found new ground. We examined how early psychologists were intrigued by the potential for behaviors and psychological traits to be inherited, an idea that persisted even as genetics began to provide more concrete explanations for biological inheritance.

In more recent times, we explored contemporary perspectives that have resurrected Lamarckian themes within the contexts of neuroplasticity and epigenetics, demonstrating that while Lamarck's original theories are not supported in their literal sense, the underlying principles continue to influence modern psychological science. We also discussed the potential implications of a neo-Lamarckian approach in educational psychology, suggesting that environmental and experiential learning could have generational impacts.

The Evolution of Scientific Thought

Reflecting on the changing perceptions of Lamarckian theory highlights the dynamic nature of scientific inquiry. Lamarck's ideas, once groundbreaking, then discredited, have found a new form of relevance in today's scientific discussions. This evolution in thinking underscores an important lesson about the progression of scientific theories: they are not static truths but are continually tested, challenged, and adapted as new evidence comes to light.

The case of Lamarckian theory exemplifies how scientific ideas can fall out of favor, only to be reconsidered and integrated into new frameworks as our understanding and methodologies evolve. This cyclical nature of scientific progress emphasizes the importance of maintaining an open mind and fostering a culture of ongoing inquiry and skepticism within the scientific community.

The Importance of Historical Perspectives

This book has also underscored the value of historical perspectives in evaluating scientific theories. Understanding the history of Lamarck's ideas not only enriches our appreciation of their complexity but also teaches us about the broader context of scientific discovery and the human aspects of the scientific endeavor. By studying the past, we gain insight into the processes of scientific change and continuity, learning from the trials and errors of those who came before us.

Closing Thoughts

In closing, Jean-Baptiste Lamarck's legacy in psychological science serves as a powerful reminder that ideas can transcend the time of their creation, influencing thought and research in ways the original proponents could never have imagined. Lamarck's journey from obscurity to prominence, decline, and then partial revival, offers a profound lesson on the mutable nature of science and knowledge. As we move forward, let us carry with us the spirit of inquiry and openness that Lamarck's work inspires, ever ready to reevaluate and rethink the boundaries of what we know.

As we continue to explore and understand the human mind and behavior, let Lamarckian ideas remind us of our ability to adapt—intellectually, culturally, and scientifically—to the ever-changing landscapes of knowledge and existence.

About Freudian Trips

Welcome to Freudian Trips, your dedicated platform for diving deep into the world of psychology. We are more than just a YouTube channel or a book publisher. We are a beacon of enlightenment, making complex psychological concepts accessible and engaging for all.

Our YouTube channel is a rich repository of psychology made simple. We take the profound and often complex ideas from the world of psychology and break them down into digestible, easy-to-understand content. From the foundational theories of Freud to the cognitive insights of Piaget, we cover a broad spectrum of psychological schools and thoughts, making psychology accessible to everyone, regardless of their background or prior knowledge.

As a book publisher, we take the same approach, transforming intricate psychological theories into comprehensible narratives. Our books are not just collections of words, but vessels of wisdom that make psychology approachable and relatable. We believe that psychology should not be confined to academic circles, but should be available to all who seek to understand the human mind and behavior.

At Freudian Trips, we believe in the power of curiosity and the pursuit of knowledge. We are here to stoke the fires of your curiosity, to guide you on your intellectual journey, and to help you navigate the fascinating world of psychology.

If you are someone who is not afraid to question, to explore, and to learn, then you are in the right place. Join us on this journey of exploration, as we make psychology easy to understand, one concept at a time.

Be sure to visit our Youtube channel at: www.freudiantrips.com/youtube

You can also visit us on the web at www.freudiantrips.com

Welcome to The Freudian Trip community. Stay curious. Stay enlightened.

www.ingramcontent.com/pod-product-compliance
Lightning Source LLC
Chambersburg PA
CBHW072344270726
48659CB00023B/2366